befor

Just the Facts
The Drugs Trade
Jim McGuigan

www.heinemann.co.uk/library
Visit our website to find out more information about **Heinemann Library** books.

To order:

 Phone 44 (0) 1865 888066

 Send a fax to 44 (0) 1865 314091

 Visit the Heinemann Bookshop at www.heinemann.co.uk/library to browse our catalogue and order online.

Produced by Monkey Puzzle Media Ltd
Gissing's Farm, Fressingfield, Suffolk IP21 5SH, UK

First published in Great Britain by Heinemann Library, Halley Court, Jordan Hill, Oxford OX2 8EJ, part of Harcourt Education.
Heinemann is a registered trademark of Harcourt Education Ltd.

Editorial: Clare Collinson, Sarah Eason and Louise Galpine
Design: Mayer Media Ltd
Picture Research: Lynda Lines and Frances Bailey
Production: Duncan Gilbert

Originated by Ambassador Litho Ltd
Printed and bound in Hong Kong, China by South China Printing Company

ISBN 0 431 16177 1
09 08 07 06 05
10 9 8 7 6 5 4 3 2 1

British Library Cataloguing in Publication Data
McGuigan, Jim
The Drugs Trade
363.4'5
A full catalogue record for this book is available from the British Library.

Acknowledgements
The publishers would like to thank the following for permission to reproduce photographs:
AKG-Images p. **6**; Alamy pp. **15 bottom** (David Hoffman Photo Library), **20** (Image 100), **26** (Mikael Karlsson); Associated Press pp. **16–17** (B K Bangash), **31** (Scott Dalton), **43**; Camera Press p. **45** (Gary Doak); Corbis pp. **4** (Scott Houston), **8**, **10–11** (Tom and Dee Ann McCarthy), **18** (Joe Klein/Sygma), **23** (Rick Gayle), **29** (Frank Trapper), **36–37** (Shelley Gazin), **40–41** (Annie Griffiths Belt), **51** (Tom and Dee Ann McCarthy); Fairtrade Foundation pp. **32** (Julia Powel), **48**; Getty Images pp. **15 top** (Banaras Khan/AFP), **41** (Fredy Amariles/AFP); Kobal Collection p. **28** (Figment/ Noel Gay/Channel 4/Longman); Panos Pictures pp. **21** (Martin Adler), **24** (Gareth Wyn Jones); Reuters pp. **19** (Daniel Aguilar), **39 top** (Hugo Philpott); Rex Features pp. **9** (SIPA), **12–13** (Sakki), **34–35** (Isopress Senepart); Science Photo Library pp. **37** (Dr Jeremy Burgess), **39 bottom** (Geoff Tompkinson), **46–47** (Sean O'Brian/Custom Medical Stock); Topham Picturepoint pp. **22** (Neil Denham), **49** (Bob Daemmrich/Image Works).

Cover photograph reproduced with permission of Reuters (Daniel Aguilar).

Every effort has been made to contact copyright holders of any material reproduced in this book. Any omissions will be rectified in subsequent printings if notice is given to the publishers.

Any words appearing in the text in bold, **like this**, are explained in the Glossary.

Contents

What is
the drugs trade?

"The illegal drugs trade brings
addiction, violence, crime and
corruption to communities all
over the world.**"**

Mr John Walters, Director of the US Office of National Drug
Policy in Washington, DC, USA

The powerful painkilling medicinal drug
oxycodone (also called hillbilly heroin) is being
traded illegally on the street. Users crush the pills
for snorting (sniffing) or boil them for injection.

A drug is any substance that a person puts in their body to change the way they feel, think or behave. A drug taken simply for pleasure is known as a **recreational drug**, whereas any drug taken for an illness or injury is a medicine. Some recreational drugs are legal and some are illegal. Tea, coffee, cola, many other soft drinks and chocolate bars all contain the legal **stimulant** drug caffeine. Other commonly taken legal drugs are alcohol and nicotine (the drug in cigarettes). There are many types of illegal drugs, including cannabis, cocaine, heroin and ecstasy. The buying and selling of illegal drugs is known as the illegal drugs trade. This book is about the illegal drugs trade.

Many different types of people are involved in the illegal drugs trade. These people are all linked together in what can be a very long chain. For a drug such as cocaine, the first link in the chain is the farmer who grows the coca plants that cocaine is made from. The farmer harvests the plants and makes them into a paste. This is sold to someone who takes it to a laboratory to be turned into a white powder, cocaine hydrochloride – the main form of cocaine that is sold to users in **Western** countries.

Drug **traffickers** pay people called carriers to hide the cocaine and smuggle it past police and customs officers so they can deliver it to drug **dealers** in different countries. The big dealers then distribute the drug to smaller dealers who sell it to drug users. And there are plenty of users: the United Nations (UN) Office for Drug Control and Crime Prevention estimates that some 200 million people around the world use illegal drugs, the most common being cannabis (also called marijuana, dope, grass and pot), with 144 million users.

A global business

The illegal drugs trade is estimated to be worth $400 billion (400 thousand million US dollars) a year, which is almost as much as the total global sales of all medical drugs ($430 billion in 2002), and amounts to 8 per cent of total worldwide trade in all goods. Two forces drive this profitable illegal business: the 'pull' from the users who want the drugs, and the 'push' from the big traffickers who supply them.

Drug use in history

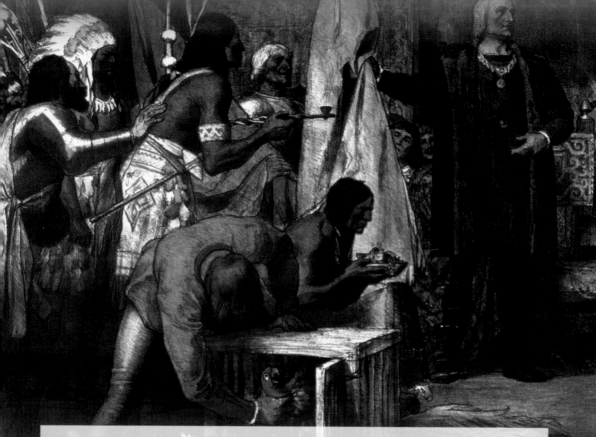

There is evidence to show that as far back as 5000 years ago people were using drugs. From Mesopotamia, the ancient region of south-west Asia now called Iraq, there are records showing that people knew about the various pain-relieving and sleep-producing effects of opium (a drug made from the opium poppy). There are many reports of other drugs being used throughout recorded history, both as medicines and also for their **stimulating** effects on the senses.

Drugs in ancient Greece

The ancient Greeks were familiar with the power of drugs. The poet Homer wrote about the use of opium in the 8th century BCE, while Hippocrates (460–377 BCE), who is considered to be the father of modern medicine, used lots of plants as medicines – including opium. Several hundred years later, another Greek doctor, called Galen (AD 130–200), wrote about the benefits of opium as a medicine.

Alcohol and tobacco

During the Middle Ages, one of the most widely used drugs was alcohol. In the 16th century, a professor in Switzerland called Paracelsus invented laudanum, a mixture of opium and alcohol. It was used a little like paracetamol is today – for sore throats, coughs and other minor illnesses. Tobacco was introduced into Europe in 1493 by the explorer Christopher Columbus and his crew returning from America.

Drugs and religious ceremonies

The ancient Greeks used **hallucinogenic** drugs in spiritual ceremonies as they thought their effects on the senses brought them closer to the spirit world. The Aztecs, who ruled Mexico from 1430 until the Spanish took over in 1521, referred to the 'sacred' mushrooms of Mexico as 'God's flesh'. When the Spanish took over the central Andes region of South America (now known as Peru) in 1535 they saw that the Inca people, who had ruled this region since 1438, chewed coca leaves as part of their religious ceremonies. This produced euphoria – a feeling or state of intense excitement and happiness – and also **hallucinations**.

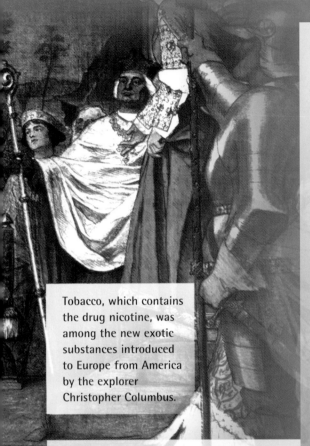

Tobacco, which contains the drug nicotine, was among the new exotic substances introduced to Europe from America by the explorer Christopher Columbus.

Cannabis

The cannabis plant is thought to have been grown first by the ancient Chinese in 2700 BCE. Its seeds were then transported to India, Africa and Europe. It has been used in Islamic countries for many centuries, especially in the form of hashish (a word which comes from an Arabic word for someone who takes the drug). The first recorded users of this form of cannabis were members of an 11th-century Islamic **sect** of murderers, known as the Assassins.

Modern history

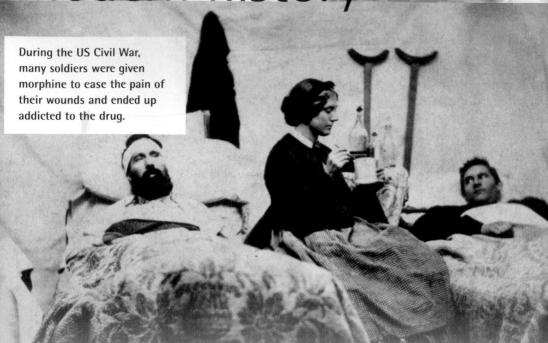

During the US Civil War, many soldiers were given morphine to ease the pain of their wounds and ended up addicted to the drug.

19th-century painkillers

Following its invention in the 16th century, laudanum was the main drug (other than alcohol) used as a medicine to treat pain, coughs and other illnesses. Its wide use continued into the 19th century. In 1805, a more powerful painkilling drug called morphine was made from opium. The invention of the hypodermic syringe (a needle used to inject drugs beneath the skin) in 1853 meant that a large number of people could be injected with morphine. More than 45,000 soldiers who were treated with morphine for injuries in the US Civil War (1861–65) became **addicted** to the drug.

Around the mid-19th century, cannabis began to be prescribed as a medical treatment for conditions such as headache and heart pain. In 1855 cocaine began to be used widely (and unsuccessfully) as a cure for morphine addiction. Further advances in chemistry gave rise in 1874 to an even stronger, highly addictive form of opium called heroin – originally advertised incorrectly as a safe, non-addictive substitute for morphine.

Many of the half-million young people who gathered at the Woodstock festival in New York state in 1969 took cannabis and other drugs.

Stimulants and hallucinogens

Amphetamines, a type of **stimulant** drug, were first synthesized (made from chemicals in a laboratory) in 1887. They were used to treat asthma and depression in the 1930s, although some people took them for the '**high**' they gave. During World War II (1939–45), troops on both sides were given amphetamines to combat tiredness. In 1943, the powerful **hallucinogenic** drug LSD (lysergic acid diethylamide) was synthesized. Doctors tried using it unsuccessfully to treat mental illness.

The 1960s onwards

By the early 1960s, some people in the USA and UK were using LSD as a **recreational drug**. The use of amphetamines among young people shot up in the 1960s and the recreational use of cannabis also became widespread at this time.

Ecstasy was first synthesized in 1912 and then largely forgotten about until the mid-1960s when Dr Alexander Shulgin, a US chemist, found a new, simple way of synthesizing it. It began to be sold in US cities in the mid-1980s, and by the late 1980s ecstasy was being used in many countries, especially by young people at dance parties called raves.

The use of illegal drugs today

At least 200 million people around the world use illegal drugs. The use of most illegal drugs is growing every year, but the biggest increase in the past ten years has been in the use of amphetamines and amphetamine-type **stimulants** (ATS).

A UN study showed that in 2002 more than 40 million people, rich and poor, and of all ages, used ATS. Police and customs officers discovered a total of 40 tonnes of ATS in 2002 – ten times the amount found in 1992. It is estimated that 500 tonnes of ATS are made in illegal laboratories (often in people's homes) every year – that is equivalent to the weight of 100 African elephants.

There are 14 million users of cocaine around the world. The drug comes mainly from Colombia, Peru and Bolivia. Colombia's trade in cocaine was worth $5 billion in 2002 compared with just $1.5 billion for one of Colombia's main legal products, coffee.

In 2002, law enforcement agencies around the world seized 5500 tonnes of cannabis – about the same weight as 15 jumbo jets, each carrying 500 passengers. This is thought to be less than a quarter of the cannabis that is being distributed.

The UK

In the UK, 12 per cent of the population aged 15–59 reported using an illegal drug during 2002. Cannabis was the most commonly used drug, followed by amphetamines, cocaine and ecstasy.

Just over one in ten of those aged 11–14 said they used cannabis, rising to almost one-third of 15-year-olds. The use of amphetamines and LSD among those aged 16–24 had fallen between 1996 and 2002, while the use of cocaine by this age group had gone up.

The USA

More than 20 million Americans reported using illegal drugs in 2002. Most of them took cannabis, while 5 million took cocaine, 4 million ATS and 1 million heroin. Recently there has been a big increase in the use of oxycodone (also called hillbilly heroin), a synthetic (manufactured in a laboratory) substitute drug for heroin.

Australia

In 2001, 38 per cent of Australians aged over 14 said that they had tried an illegal drug at least once in their life. Cannabis was the most commonly tried drug (33 per cent), followed by amphetamines (9 per cent), ecstasy (6 per cent) cocaine (4 per cent) and heroin (1.6 per cent).

Cannabis, being smoked here with tobacco, is the most commonly used illegal drug in the world.

Types of illegal drugs and their effects

Illegal drugs can be divided into three main groups: **stimulants**, **sedatives** and **hallucinogens**.

Stimulants

Stimulants, also called 'uppers', speed up the activity of the brain and make people feel alert and full of energy. They include cocaine, crack, amphetamines and ecstasy.

Cocaine (also called coke and snow) is a white powder made from the coca plant. It is usually sniffed (up the nose), and makes the user feel excited and alert

for about 20 minutes. Users also get a dry mouth, their heart beats faster, and they feel a loss of appetite. Crack (also called freebase) is a very **addictive** form of cocaine that is made into crystals and smoked. When users stop regular use of cocaine or crack they tend to feel exhausted but unable to sleep. So the urge to keep taking the drug is strong.

Amphetamines (also called speed) are laboratory-made drugs, sold mainly as pills or as a white powder. Each dose of the powder is contained in a small piece of paper known as a wrap.

The powder is usually taken by dissolving it in a soft or alcoholic drink or in a cup of tea. Sometimes it is dissolved in water and injected. Breathing and heart rates quicken after taking the drug and the user feels more energetic. The effects last for 3–4 hours. Amphetamines raise the blood pressure, which may increase the risk of heart problems. Large doses and regular use can lead to feelings of anxiety and **paranoia**.

Ecstasy (also called E or **MDMA**) is an amphetamine-type drug which also has mild hallucinogenic effects. Ecstasy can be obtained as a tablet or capsule in a huge range of sizes and colours. The effects start after 20–60 minutes and can last several hours. Users often take ecstasy at dance clubs or raves, saying that it gives them energy, confidence and a peaceful closeness to their friends. Physical effects include sweating, a dry mouth, feeling sick and increased heart rate. Some people feel anxious and panicky after taking ecstasy. Regular use of ecstasy may lead to sleep problems, lack of energy and depression. There have been a small number of deaths associated with the use of ecstasy. As it is a relatively new drug, its long-term effects are not yet known.

The smiley face is a common imprint on ecstasy tablets; also typical is the outline of a dove or the letter 'E'.

Sedatives

Sedative drugs slow down the brain and make people feel relaxed, sleepy and in some cases separated from the rest of the world. Many sedative drugs are known as opiates because they are derived from the opium poppy. The main opiates are heroin (also called smack) and morphine, which is often used to control severe pain in people with cancer. Heroin comes in various forms and can be injected, smoked, sniffed, or heated on foil and the fumes inhaled. The effects, which include feelings of contentment, relaxation and drowsiness, can last for several hours. Regular use of heroin can quickly lead to a serious physical addiction.

Hallucinogens

Hallucinogenic drugs affect the way people see, hear, feel, smell or touch the world. People who use them may see colours much more brightly or hear sounds differently.

Lysergic acid diethylamide (LSD) (also called acid) is a laboratory-made drug that causes **hallucinations**. It is usually put into pills, capsules or blotter paper. The effects of LSD begin about 30 minutes after taking the drug and can last up to 12 hours. In some cases users experience a bad '**trip**', in which they see frightening visions and feel panic, paranoia and depression.

Magic mushrooms grow in many parts of the world, and are also supplied dried or in tablets. They contain the drug psilocybin. The effects are similar to a mild dose of LSD. Probably the biggest danger from trying this drug is that someone might eat a poisonous mushroom by mistake.

2CB and 2Ci are hallucinogenic drugs related to ecstasy, and have similar effects and side effects as ecstasy. The drugs are sold either as a white powder or as small pills.

Cannabis

Cannabis is a drug that does not fit into any of the above groups. It comes from the plant *Cannabis sativa*, which grows all over the world. There are two common sorts of cannabis: the dry leaves usually known as grass, and a black or dark brown resin. Cannabis is usually smoked or put into cakes and biscuits. The drug can make people more relaxed, dreamy, giggly and talkative; it can also make them feel anxious and nervy. Studies of cannabis use show that it makes the memory less reliable and many experts believe it

These packets of heroin were found buried in a secret dump in Pakistan, close to the border with Afghanistan.

reduces concentration. Cannabis is often smoked mixed with tobacco, which can increase a person's risk of developing cancer. Cannabis may be psychologically addictive, and some experts believe that long-term use may make people withdrawn and more susceptible to mental illness.

Strips of blotter paper containing the drug LSD. The paper is usually printed with cartoon-style pictures.

Where do illegal drugs come from?

An estimated 4 million people depend on income derived from growing illegal drug crops such as the coca plant and opium poppy. Most are very poor people who receive about half of their income from drug-crop cultivation. Although the drugs trade often provides enough money for them to cope with food shortages, it leaves them with a very uncertain long-term future. Because their crops are illegal, these farmers are unable to get any support from the government if they get into difficulties.

Cocaine

About 600 tonnes of cocaine are produced in Colombia each year – about three-quarters of the world's supply. The rest comes from Peru and Bolivia to make a total of 800 tonnes – more than three times the weight of the US Statue of Liberty. Many farmers in these countries work on farms that are owned by drug **traffickers**. The farmers live in constant fear of being forced by the government to stop growing their illegal

Farmers harvesting opium poppies (used to make heroin) in Chapliar, Afghanistan.

crop. Given suitable alternatives, most farmers would gladly switch to other sources of income. But they need government help to do this, or the traffickers entice or bully them back into growing drug crops.

Heroin

The main opium-growing region in the world is Afghanistan. In 2002, 180,000 hectares of land – enough to make 1800 championship golf courses – were used for growing opium poppies.

This brought a harvest of some 4500 tonnes of opium, which is the equivalent of 450 tonnes of pure heroin. Afghanistan is the source of about 75 per cent of the world's heroin and 90 per cent of the heroin that reaches the UK.

Cannabis

Cannabis crops are grown in more than 100 different countries. Morocco, Afghanistan, Pakistan and the West Indies are thought to be the main sources of the drug, but large amounts are also grown in the USA and in European countries such as the Netherlands.

Amphetamine-type substances (ATS)

ATS such as ecstasy are chemical drugs that can be produced simply and cheaply in 'kitchen laboratories' close to where the drugs are sold. The Internet is blamed for the rapid spread of knowledge of how to set up such laboratories. Around 12,000 labs around the world were dismantled in 2002 by the police. Some labs can produce a million ecstasy tablets a week. ATS are sold for 30 to 40 times more than it costs to make them. The high profits make the ATS business very attractive to criminal gangs.

How are illegal drugs distributed?

The trade in illegal drugs involves a huge international distribution network, which transports drugs from the grower to the user. And it has never been easier or cheaper to travel: there are more planes, boats, trucks and people to carry drugs from one part of the world to another than ever before.

cartel traffickers all have the latest radios and other communication equipment to help them stay one step ahead of the police and customs officers who are trying to catch them. They also have the latest guns and other weapons to deal with anyone who gets in their way.

Cartel traffickers

The bosses in charge of large-scale drug **trafficking** are called cartel traffickers. A cartel is an association of different traffickers who all agree to sell illegal drugs for the same high price. These

Carriers

Cartel traffickers pay other people to do the risky work of trying to sneak illegal drugs past customs officers into another country. These people, called carriers or mules, can be very good at concealing

A huge illegal shipment of cocaine found on a cargo boat arriving in the USA.

618   U.S. COA

drugs in all sorts of everyday belongings – from tubes of toothpaste and bars of chocolate to camera tripod stands. They may also try to hide drugs inside their bodies, by wrapping the drugs in rubber or plastic and swallowing them. They wait until the drugs pass right through their bodies and into a toilet bowl before they can recover them. Many carriers are arrested at ports and airports, and put in jail or deported (sent back to their own country); others may die because the bag of drugs they swallowed burst inside them.

Transporting drugs

Drug traffickers also organize huge shipments of many tonnes of illegal drugs to be smuggled into countries such as the USA, the UK and other European countries. Many of the illegal drugs sold in the UK arrive secretly on boats travelling between large ports such as Southampton and Rotterdam. But drugs also enter the UK in small (a few kilos) to medium (tens of kilos) quantities in cars that arrive by ferry.

Mexico is one of the main 'gateways' for illegal drugs going into the USA. Colombian traffickers transport drugs to Mexico by boat. Mexican traffickers then transport the drugs to the US border. The drugs then travel by road, rail, or commercial airline to major US cities.

The traffickers strike deals with criminal organizations in each country to transport the drugs and distribute them to **dealers** who sell them to drug users.

A Mexican policeman searching for drugs in Culiacán, in the state of Sinaloa. One of the main routes for drugs entering the USA is across the Mexican border.

Who takes illegal drugs?

All types of people use drugs illegally: doctors, teachers, social workers, government ministers, police officers, soldiers, and at least one bishop. A recent study found that more than one in ten of all UK employees use illegal drugs. Illegal drug use among doctors is higher than among many other groups of workers. One reason is that many types of illegal drugs have a medical form, so doctors are easily able to get hold of them.

Studies show that men are more likely generally to use illegal drugs than women, single people more than married people, city-dwellers more than country people, and younger people more than older people. Use of illegal drugs is also very common among people in prison. In **developed countries**, many of the people who use illegal drugs are people with homes and jobs. In **developing countries** many drug users are very poor people, often children, living on the street or in temporary shelters.

Some recent surveys suggest that more young women than young men may be experimenting with illegal drugs. This may be because girls mature earlier, mix with boys who are older and so come into contact with drugs at an earlier age than boys.

Lines of cocaine, ready to be snorted at a party.

Work and drugs

A UK government-sponsored study by Cardiff University in 2004 found that:

- 13 per cent of employees reported using illegal drugs in the previous year
- use of illegal drugs decreased with age, from 29 per cent of those under 30 to 3 per cent of those over 50
- minor injuries at work were more common among illegal drug users.

A young heroin user in Lisbon, Portugal, prepares his syringe, while another injects himself with the drug.

Case study Rob's story

Rob was 13 when he first tried cannabis. He smoked it inside roll-up cigarettes. A lot of older boys at his school were smoking it. He says, 'I wanted to know what it was like. It made me feel relaxed and wanting to laugh at things. Nobody, like teachers and parents, knew what we were doing; it was cool.'

'Sometimes it was a bit scary and I got **paranoid**. Once I was smoking at my friend's house, and I went to the toilet. I felt sick and I thought I could see sort of squid tentacles with suckers on them coming out of the toilet pan.'

Rob said he stopped smoking because it made him feel sick and dizzy. He also said he was scared of getting cancer from the cigarette smoke.

The impact of drugs on the individual

Recreational drug use

Some people take drugs socially or **recreationally**. They use drugs regularly for fun, often at weekends, over many months or years. They learn quite a lot about drugs and are fussy about the type they buy, and the way they use them. While these people tend not to be **addicted** to drugs, they have made them a part of their life and accept the tiredness and low mood that often follows a night of drug-taking. It can take years before they 'step back' and see what impact their drug habit is having on their lives.

Some people use drugs such as ecstasy only at weekends, when they go clubbing. Studies have shown that some ecstasy users suffer a range of long-term problems, including memory loss, anxiety, impulsive behaviour and depression. These effects are thought to be due to the fact that ecstasy interferes with the levels of the chemical serotonin in the brain. Serotonin plays an important part in regulating mood and memory.

Some people feel they need ecstasy to have a good time when they go clubbing.

Case study Steve's story

Steve was 16, living with his parents and working in the computer industry when he first took ecstasy – a friend offered him some, telling him what it was like.

Steve remembers feeling uncontrollable excitement and happiness and energy when he took ecstasy. 'I didn't know what I wanted to do, whether I wanted to sit down, get up, dance, walk about, or just sit in a corner by myself. Me and my pal were standing in the middle of the dance floor laughing like mad at each other. Then I got dizzy and felt sick. But it wore off and I got up and started dancing again, and we went on till two in the morning.'

Steve began to realize that over the months, the drug was taking it out of him. 'Sundays were the worst. It can make you really depressed and going back to work is unbearable. You don't get your head together until about Tuesday. I made a decision to stop taking E. It didn't work for me any more; it was just a habit, and I was starting to feel down about it. There was nothing else in my life to make me feel that bad, so the drug must have caused it.'

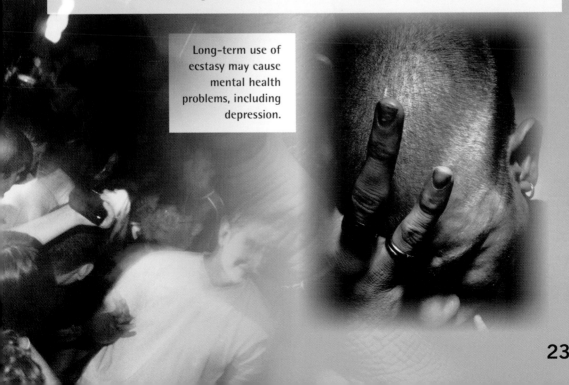

Long-term use of ecstasy may cause mental health problems, including depression.

Drug dependence

Drug **dependence** is when someone feels they have to continue taking a drug to feel OK or to avoid feeling bad. They may have become physically dependent on (or addicted to) the drug and they become ill if they stop taking it. Heroin, nicotine and alcohol are all examples of drugs that people can become physically dependent on. People who stop taking heroin, for example, suffer a range of symptoms including aching muscles, severe cramps and stiff joints. Some people also become psychologically addicted to drugs – if they stop, they do not feel physical discomfort, but the lack of the drug

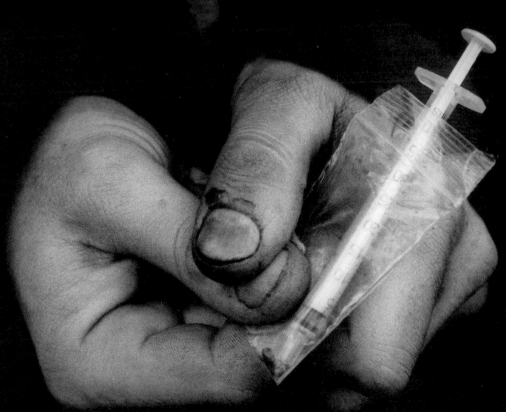

In the grip of heroin addiction: a syringe is kept close at hand.

plays on their mind, making them go back for more.

The effects of drug dependence

Physical drug dependence usually affects a person's day-to-day life. People who are physically dependent on drugs tend to stay around other people who are dependent on the same drug. Often they will run out of money to buy drugs and may turn to crime to get more money. They may fall out with their families and some may sell their bodies for sex – getting paid in money or with drugs. This puts them at risk from disease and violence.

Case study Sarah's story

'I thought it would take ages, years before I got addicted, 'cos I've got strong will power. But I got on to it really quickly.' Sarah had got the heroin from her boyfriend who was hooked on the drug and had tried to keep it away from her. 'You can hide it at first, find ways of covering up but later you don't care – how you look, what you do. I was stealing off my mum – taking money and selling jewellery and clothes.'

'At first my family didn't notice, then my mum knew something was wrong – noticed how sneaky I was, stealing money, an' that.' Sarah said she started to lose respect for herself, and eventually none of her family would speak to her.

Sarah's first baby was born heroin-dependent – it had been exposed to the heroin that was in Sarah's bloodstream while it was growing inside her. It was when the doctors had to treat the baby for the effects of heroin that Sarah's parents first found out that she was addicted to the drug.

'I stopped with the shock of having my baby taken off me. I had reached the pits, I was banging my head on the wall, feeling really suicidal: it was go into **rehab** or die.'

The impact of drugs on society

Illegal drug use does not just affect the life of the person using the drugs – the local community is also affected and there are wider reaching effects on society as a whole.

Many thefts and violent attacks on people are by drug users desperate to get money for drugs. Governments have to spend money on coping with drug-related crimes, leaving less money for tackling other crimes. Buying drugs on the street helps the big international **traffickers** to stay in business, making sure that drug-related crime and suffering continues around the world. Drug-related problems also include increased susceptibility to **AIDS** and the liver disease hepatitis (owing to sharing syringe needles with others who have these illnesses). This leads to increased demand for medical treatment.

A man is arrested for selling crack cocaine; another drug dealer is likely to quickly take his place.

The UK

Illegal drug use caused businesses in the UK to lose an estimated £800 million in 2001, because of days off work, poor judgement and lack of concentration. A report from the UK's National Association for the Care and Resettlement of Offenders (1999) says that one in three thefts, burglaries and other street robberies in the UK is related to drugs.

Someone **addicted** to heroin on average spends about £10,000 a year on the drug, while crack users spend an average of £20,000 a year. Much of the money used to buy illegal drugs comes from crime. Drug-related violent crime – usually involving battles between rival drug-dealing gangs – is on the increase.

The USA

It has been estimated that illegal drug-taking by the US workforce costs industry about $15 billion dollars a year. An estimated 61,000 (16 per cent) of convicted jail inmates committed their offence to obtain money for drugs (US Bureau of Justice Statistics, 2000). Of 13,752 murders in 2001, 4 per cent were drug-related.

Australia

In 1998 in Australia there were 1023 drug-related deaths. While this is a worryingly high number, it looks small when compared with the 19,000 deaths caused in the same year by tobacco smoking and the 2400 deaths that were due to alcohol consumption. (The same patterns of high death rates from cigarette smoking and alcohol, compared with illegal drugs, are seen in the USA, UK and many other countries.)

"Amphetamines may cause dependence and psychoses. Ecstasy may speed up the normal ageing process ... Who will assist, and pay for, a generation of abusers under-performing in schools and at work because of the impact of abuse?"

Antonio Maria Costa, Executive Director of the UN Office on Drugs and Crime (UNODC)

Drugs and the media

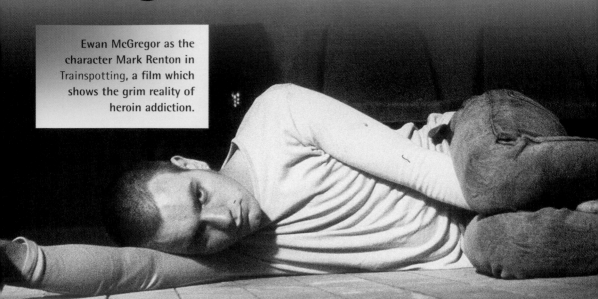

Ewan McGregor as the character Mark Renton in Trainspotting, a film which shows the grim reality of heroin addiction.

The media – television, radio, newspapers and magazines – influences the way people think about drugs.

Print media

Many newspapers, especially **tabloids**, print sensationalized (exaggerated and distorted) stories about illegal drug users, simply to sell more copies. They use headlines such as 'Cannabis-crazed fiend breaks into surgery' or 'Ecstasy will rot your brain.' When young people see these exaggerated news reports, it may make them distrust information from the media and from others mentioned in the media such as police officers and politicians. Young people are less likely to follow advice about illegal drugs from such sources if they do not trust them to tell the truth.

Television and films

Television programmes aimed at teenagers rarely show illegal drugs being taken. However, a recent US study showed that illegal drugs were mentioned in 21 per cent of a sample of episodes from the situation comedies and dramas that are most popular with US teenagers. The downside of taking drugs was shown much more than any positive side to taking drugs.

On the rare occasions that children's programmes show illegal drugs being used, they tend to portray the most extreme **stereotypical** cases. An exception to this is the British drama series called Grange Hill, set in a

Drugs and celebrities

The media often glamorizes drug-taking by the rich and famous. But sometimes a celebrity talking about their drug problem can encourage people to admit to their own problem and seek help. Ozzy Osbourne, for example, has spoken openly about his drug use and more recently his son Jack has gone on air to talk about his treatment for addiction to oxycodone (hillbilly heroin).

Media coverage is not always sensationalized. The drug-related death in 1994 of Kurt Cobain, of the pop group Nirvana, was reported carefully by the local media in Seattle, USA. Each news report was edited to ensure that the singer's musical achievements were separated from his drug-taking.

secondary school. It ran a storyline involving a heroin **addict**, and effectively put over the difficult issues involved.

TV soaps such as *Eastenders*, *Coronation Street* and *Neighbours*, which are watched by massive international audiences, also tend to show only the very extreme cases of drug use. The reality of millions of young people using ecstasy every week at dance clubs around the world is largely ignored.

A recent US study of movies and popular TV dramas and comedy shows reported that movies are more than five times more likely to show illegal drug-taking than TV programmes.

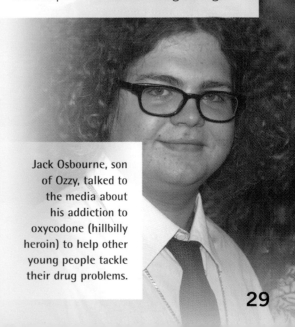

Jack Osbourne, son of Ozzy, talked to the media about his addiction to oxycodone (hillbilly heroin) to help other young people tackle their drug problems.

Why is there a drugs trade?

The reasons for the thriving trade in illegal drugs are complex. The 'needs and wants' of the drug users help to drive the trade in illegal drugs. But equally important are the 'needs and wants' of those who grow or manufacture the drugs.

Why do people grow drugs crops?

Many illegal drugs are produced in the world's poorest countries, such as Colombia and Afghanistan. This is partly because these countries offer the right growing conditions for the plants from which the drugs are made. But it is also because many people in these countries live in poverty and are not able to earn enough money through selling legal goods to achieve a decent standard of living.

Rural poverty

Many people in rural areas in **developing countries** rely on the small patches of land they own to provide food and money. But for a range of reasons, including wars and severe lack of rainwater (drought), these people often cannot earn a living from the land. Some find it is expensive to transport their food crops to the towns and cities to be sold for export. When trying to sell their goods, it is hard for them to compete with farmers in **developed countries** who have the technology to grow foods more efficiently and transport them more cheaply. Since many farmers have soil that is good for growing drug crops, some are changing over to drug-crop cultivation as an easier way to make money.

❝Compared with food cash crops, drug crops provide a higher level of income to poor rural communities. Rural farmers need to be offered alternatives, through national development programmes, that could achieve similar income levels.❞

Tiffany Gordon, Social Development Specialist, Latin America

Case study Coca in Colombia

During the past 70 years, large landowners in Colombia have taken over more land. This has forced people in the countryside to try to earn a living from smaller and smaller pieces of land. Many have survived by growing coffee plants but increasing competition from other countries meant that, by the late 1980s, many Colombian farmers could no longer earn enough from this crop. Some realized that they could earn more money by growing coca plants to be made into cocaine. Between 1990 and 2000 coffee production fell by 25 per cent, while coca plant production almost doubled.

From one hectare of land used to grow coffee plants, a Colombian farmer can earn £200, compared with £1700 if the land is used to grow coca plants for cocaine.

The globalization of agriculture

The growth of international trading (the buying and selling of goods between countries) of foods is part of a process called the globalization of agriculture. Different countries all try to get the best price for their products, but because developed countries decided the rules for international trade, many farmers in

This Costa Rican farmer is sure to get a fair price for his coffee thanks to trading agreements set up by the Fairtrade Foundation.

developing countries do not get a fair price for their products (such as coffee or bananas) when they sell them to developed countries.

Non-governmental organizations (NGOs), such as Oxfam and Traidcraft, are putting pressure on the governments of developed countries to set up **fair trade** practices, so that farmers in developing countries receive a fair price for their products. But not enough farmers are currently benefiting from these fair trade practices.

Debts

Developing countries owe huge sums of money to developed countries and many poor countries struggle to repay these debts. Some are forced to grow large amounts of particular crops (called cash crops) to sell to other countries rather than to feed their own hungry people. Debts put developing countries in a weak position to negotiate a fair price for their goods.

When faced with unfair trade rules and huge debts, some poor countries turn to growing plants that can be sold to make illegal drugs.

'War on drugs'

The illegal drugs trade may be made more profitable by enforcement of the very laws that were set up to wipe it out. Total outlawing of a drug, also called **prohibition**, was attempted in the USA between 1920 and 1933 to stop alcohol **abuse**, but it failed miserably as alcohol-related crimes rose. The USA's current 'war on drugs' (see page 42) attempts to cut off the supply of drugs, but a reduction in drug supply can push up the prices paid by the users, so the **traffickers** and **dealers** make even more money.

Terrorists and criminal gangs

Some terrorists and criminal gangs rely on profits from illegal drugs. Terrorists play an important part in ensuring that the drugs trade continues to thrive: for example, terrorists operating in Afghanistan control areas with huge fields of opium poppies, and protect the growers from interference by law enforcement agencies. The terrorists receive money from the heroin traffickers, who belong to large criminal organizations that make their money distributing the heroin around the world.

Why do young people take drugs?

There are many different reasons why young people take illegal drugs. Youth is a time of growth, of change, of trying new experiences such as skateboarding, horse riding, canoeing – all of which have risks. For some young people, drugs are another new and pleasurable thing to experiment with. Others may be drawn into trying drugs because they are bored, have no job, and feel their local community offers them little to do. Rebellion against parents and teachers can be a force that leads some young people to take drugs.

A young person's relationship with their parents or guardians can have an influence on their approach to illegal drugs. They may use drugs to escape from a hurtful relationship.

Peer pressure

Some young people first try drugs when their friends persuade them to do so. To refuse would mean being left out, and most young people don't want to miss out on new experiences with their friends. Young people who feel positive about themselves, believe in their self worth and feel optimistic about their future, find it easier to resist **peer pressure** regarding drugs.

The media

The media is also a big influence on young people: television, radio and magazines aimed at teenagers regularly mention drugs and celebrities who take drugs. Song lyrics frequently refer to drugs in a way that suggests they are 'cool'.

Look-alike pills

Some high-street shops sell mildly stimulating herbs as look-alike ecstasy

Sharing a roll-up of cannabis and tobacco (joint): another new experience in growing up or a deliberate rebellion?

pills. These pills may plant the idea of taking drugs in the minds of young people as they wander through the shopping mall. Having taken a 'pretend' ecstasy tablet, they may be more ready to take a real one.

Drugs on the Internet

The Internet is a powerful source of information about all aspects of drugs. A simple Internet search will turn up dozens of websites that allow people to order illegal drugs, especially opiates, for home-delivery. Open and honest communication between young people and their parents is vital to reduce the risks from inaccurate information obtained on the Internet. Young people should be warned to steer clear of the huge numbers of websites that contain incorrect information on drugs. It is also important that they understand the dangers of giving their personal details to anyone they 'meet' on the Internet.

Legal issues

Most countries around the world have laws to control the use of illegal drugs. In some countries people who break drugs laws even face the death penalty.

UK

The UK Misuse of Drugs Act 1971 treats **Class A drugs** as the most dangerous, **Class B** next most dangerous, and **Class C** the least dangerous. The more dangerous the drug is considered, the higher the penalties. As in other countries, selling to others always gets a person in more trouble than if the drugs are just for their own use.

Sometimes new evidence about a drug means it is moved from a high danger to a lower danger group. For example, in the UK in January 2004, cannabis was re-classified from Class B to Class C. That takes it out of the category which includes amphetamines and places it in the same category as sleeping pills and some painkilling medicines.

USA

Each US state has its own laws about illegal drugs. But there are also federal laws (laws which apply over the whole of the USA). Even if a state law allows cannabis to be used as a medicine, a person can still be charged under the federal law, which states that all types of cannabis use are illegal.

Australia

Laws regarding illegal drug use vary from state to state, and are also governed by various federal laws. While cannabis is illegal, someone caught with a small amount for the first time is usually not arrested but only cautioned (warned) by the police. But the law is tough on the

drug **traffickers**, who face 25 years in prison if caught.

The Netherlands

Laws here are based on the concept of **harm reduction**: that is, to minimize the health risks of drug use rather than trying to ban all drugs. Certain coffee shops are allowed to sell small amounts of cannabis to people over the age of 18. The aim is to discourage people from going to **dealers** who might also try to sell them more dangerous drugs such as heroin.

Classifying drugs

Class A drugs include: cocaine, heroin, crack, LSD, morphine, ecstasy and any Class B drug prepared for injection.

Class B drugs include: amphetamines, codeine (a painkiller derived from morphine) and other weaker medicinal drugs derived from the opium poppy.

Class C drugs include: tranquillizers such as diazepam (Valium) and temazepam, mild amphetamines, some painkilling medicines and cannabis (from 2004).

Using illegal drugs can land a young person in prison.

Packets of cannabis seeds offered for sale in a street market in Amsterdam, the Netherlands.

Legalizing cannabis: the cases for and against

Many people in Europe, Australia and the USA believe that the laws concerning illegal drugs should be changed. Most of these people think that taking cannabis should be legalized – that is, no longer a crime. If we legalize cannabis we are saying that cannabis is safe enough to buy and use in the same way as alcohol and cigarettes. This would be wrong according to another large group of people who are strongly against the legalization of cannabis.

Arguments for

The arguments for legalizing cannabis include:

- the penalties for using cannabis or supplying it to someone else – criminal record, time in jail – are considered by many people to be more damaging in the long term than the drug itself

- more than 90 per cent of all drug offences in the UK and USA involve cannabis; if police could ignore cannabis use, they could spend their time dealing with the trade in more dangerous drugs and the violent crime linked to that trade

- studies of the effects of cannabis on the body have found that it causes few harmful effects – far fewer than are caused by alcohol and cigarettes

- studies carried out over the past 100 years show that the easy availability of a drug does not mean that people suddenly start to use it in huge uncontrolled amounts.

Celebrity supporters of the case for legalizing cannabis include former Beatles member Sir Paul McCartney, and the Reverend Richard Holloway, former Bishop of Edinburgh.

Arguments against

The arguments against legalizing cannabis include:

- smoking cannabis puts people at risk of lung cancer and other smoking-related illnesses because cannabis is often smoked with tobacco

- making cannabis use easier will mean more young people will use it and move on to try more dangerous drugs such as heroin

- some studies suggest that cannabis use can trigger mental illness such as **schizophrenia**.

The law in the UK changed in January 2004. Cannabis was downgraded from a **Class B** drug to a **Class C** drug. However, people caught in possession with intent to supply, and those caught dealing in cannabis will, if convicted, still face a sentence of a maximum of fourteen years' imprisonment and an unlimited fine – the same maximum sentence as given for a Class B drug offence.

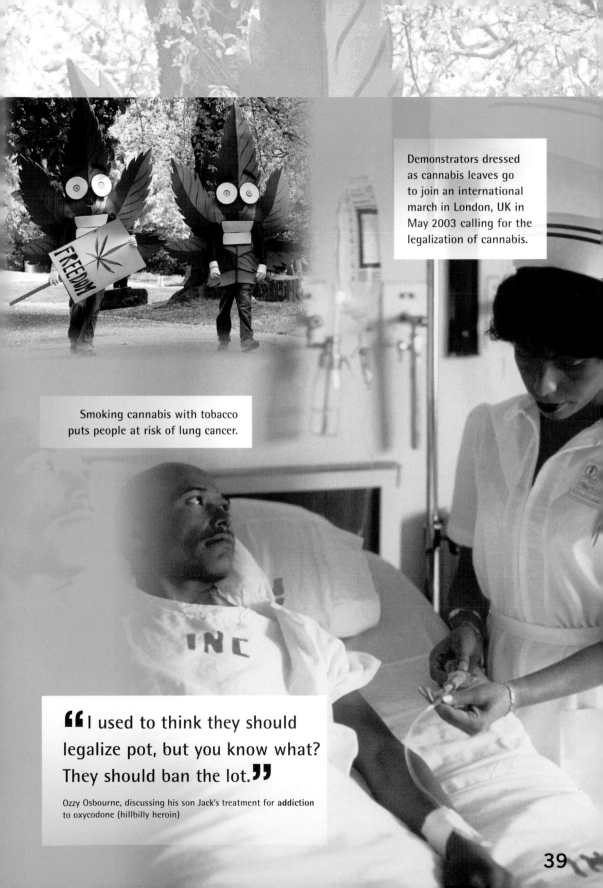

Demonstrators dressed as cannabis leaves go to join an international march in London, UK in May 2003 calling for the legalization of cannabis.

FREEDOM

Smoking cannabis with tobacco puts people at risk of lung cancer.

❝I used to think they should legalize pot, but you know what? They should ban the lot.❞

Ozzy Osbourne, discussing his son Jack's treatment for addiction to oxycodone (hillbilly heroin)

Tackling the drugs trade

The United Nations

One of the most important organizations involved in tackling illegal drugs is the United Nations (UN), an international organization of countries set up in 1945 to promote international peace, security and cooperation. One of the major concerns of the UN is to try to reduce the worldwide growth in the trade in illegal drugs.

The UN's 191 member countries have pledged that by 2008 they will have eliminated or greatly reduced the growth of drug crops used to make cocaine, cannabis and heroin.

After a terrorist attack on the USA on 11 September 2001, the UN Security Council unanimously made Resolution 1373. This requires that every member country takes steps to prevent the financing of terrorism by the sale of illegal drugs. The UN strategy is to fight both the demand for and the supply of drugs. It aims to reduce demand by educating young people about drugs.

A volunteer collects used syringes as part of a scheme to give clean needles to injecting drug users in Vancouver, Canada. The fewer people that use the same needle, the lower the risk of spreading diseases such as AIDS.

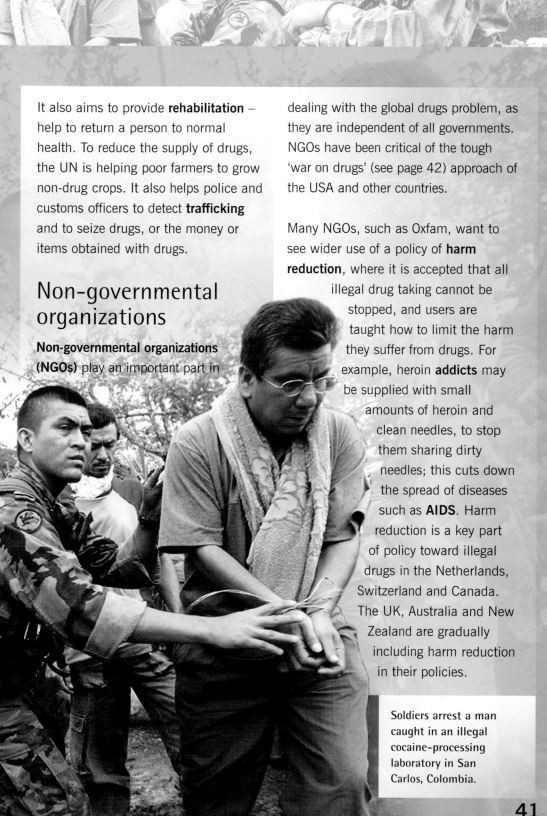

It also aims to provide **rehabilitation** – help to return a person to normal health. To reduce the supply of drugs, the UN is helping poor farmers to grow non-drug crops. It also helps police and customs officers to detect **trafficking** and to seize drugs, or the money or items obtained with drugs.

Non-governmental organizations

Non-governmental organizations (NGOs) play an important part in dealing with the global drugs problem, as they are independent of all governments. NGOs have been critical of the tough 'war on drugs' (see page 42) approach of the USA and other countries.

Many NGOs, such as Oxfam, want to see wider use of a policy of **harm reduction**, where it is accepted that all illegal drug taking cannot be stopped, and users are taught how to limit the harm they suffer from drugs. For example, heroin **addicts** may be supplied with small amounts of heroin and clean needles, to stop them sharing dirty needles; this cuts down the spread of diseases such as **AIDS**. Harm reduction is a key part of policy toward illegal drugs in the Netherlands, Switzerland and Canada. The UK, Australia and New Zealand are gradually including harm reduction in their policies.

Soldiers arrest a man caught in an illegal cocaine-processing laboratory in San Carlos, Colombia.

41

National governments

Every country has its own particular illegal drugs problem, and is best suited to finding a solution – usually working to fit in with international policies established by the UN. Powerful **developed countries** such as the USA play a part in the way **developing countries** deal with their drugs problem.

The USA

The USA has declared a 'war on drugs'. To reduce the demand for drugs, it takes a very tough approach to drug taking, and thousands of people are imprisoned each year for drug offences. In a recent US media campaign, child actors appeared on television posing as drug users who admitted that because they bought illegal drugs they were helping to fund terrorism.

Tough methods are also used to reduce the supply of drugs. Hundreds of millions of dollars are spent sending helicopters and advisers to Colombia and other South American countries to destroy coca crops to try and cut off the supply of cocaine. Some people say this does not work: instead of removing drugs from the streets, it just pushes up the prices, causes more crime by drug users desperate for drugs, and makes the **dealers** even richer.

The UK

From December 2002, a new plan for tackling illegal drugs meant a sharper focus on drugs such as cocaine and heroin. Harm reduction is an important part of the plan, which includes giving small amounts of heroin to those users who would benefit from it. New community treatment services have been established, which aim to reduce the risk of offenders returning to drugs when they come out of prison.

Australia

In Australia, harm reduction methods are being used more and more for dealing with the drugs problem. Some states recently began providing rooms where heroin users can safely inject the drug. However the federal government, whose laws apply over the whole country, has disapproved of such schemes and may stop them.

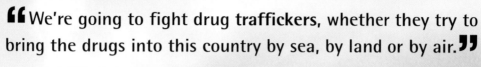

" We're going to fight drug **traffickers**, whether they try to bring the drugs into this country by sea, by land or by air. **"**

George W Bush, US President, announcing the new national drug control strategy in February 2002

Anti-drugs officers use a Blackhawk helicopter donated by the USA to burn an illegal cocaine-processing laboratory in Tibu, north-east Colombia.

The role of religious groups and the media

Christianity

Some church leaders take a firm anti-drug taking line. For example, Pope John Paul II said that using illegal drugs not only damages our health but also frustrates our capacity to live together and to help others.

Other church representatives say that the widespread acceptance of drug-taking by society must be challenged. 'It is a major cause of death and social disorder and has a destructive influence on Australia's young people,' said Bishop Patrick Power at a recent conference on the drugs problem. The drugs problem, he said, should be viewed more as a health and social problem than a matter of crime. He wants to see alternative measures to imprisonment, and more money being spent on treatment and **rehabilitation**.

Some church leaders, such as the former bishop of Edinburgh, Scotland, the Reverend Richard Holloway, take a view of drug use that has led to newspaper headlines calling them 'pulpit drug-pushers'. These religious leaders think that young users should be helped by being taught how to use certain illegal drugs responsibly and moderately.

Other religions

Intoxicating the body with drugs, especially alcohol, goes against the Muslim faith, while the Jewish, Hindu and many other faiths have clear rules banning or limiting exposure to drugs.

On the other hand, drugs are taken as part of the rituals of some religions. For example, **Rastafarians** smoke cannabis as part of their religious customs.

Media

The media has an important role to play in reporting drugs issues in a non-judgemental way. This means taking care with language, using neutral words such as 'drug user' instead of 'junkie'. Otherwise a divided culture of 'them' (the drug users) and 'us' (the non-drug users) is created.

Direct action by media groups

Some media groups run campaigns to educate teenagers and highlight the dangers of drug use. For example, the Partnership for a Drug-Free America is a private group of media professionals who donate time and money towards such campaigns.

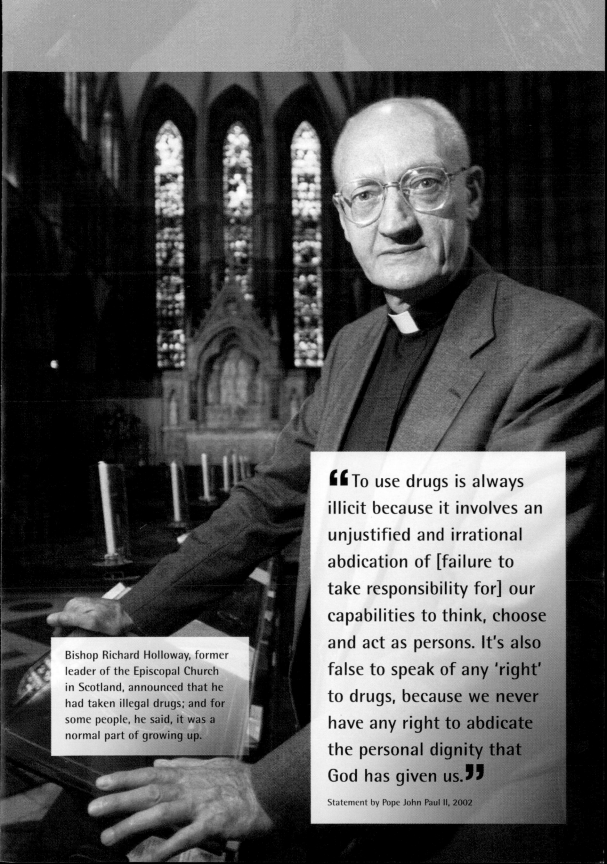

Bishop Richard Holloway, former leader of the Episcopal Church in Scotland, announced that he had taken illegal drugs; and for some people, he said, it was a normal part of growing up.

❝To use drugs is always illicit because it involves an unjustified and irrational abdication of [failure to take responsibility for] our capabilities to think, choose and act as persons. It's also false to speak of any 'right' to drugs, because we never have any right to abdicate the personal dignity that God has given us.❞

Statement by Pope John Paul II, 2002

Drug awareness and open dialogue

It is important for people to be aware of the main laws regarding drugs in the country in which they live or in countries they travel to. Films and other media can give a false impression that drugs such as cannabis can be taken without getting into trouble with the police. This is far from true.

clear set of rules about the use of alcohol, cigarettes and drugs. A young person is more likely to use drugs when parents put across mixed messages: for example, when a mother tells her teenage son never to come home drunk, while she regularly gets drunk herself.

Importance of open dialogue with parents

The chance of becoming dependent on drugs, having tried them once or twice, depends largely on a person's home environment. It is less likely to happen in homes where a young person is able to talk truthfully and openly with their parents, and is aware of a

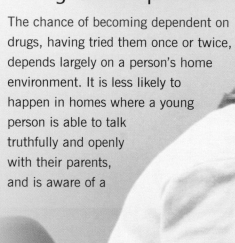

Coming off drugs

People trying to beat an **addiction** to drugs often find it useful to focus on something that they have always wanted to do – whether it is learning practical skills in plumbing, writing poems or returning to college to strengthen their general education. The good feeling of being in control that results from stopping a drug can give someone's confidence a much-needed boost.

If young people need help regarding drugs, their parents or teachers may be able to help. Another option is to call a free confidential helpline, such as the UK's Talk to Frank. Trained counsellors will then talk people through the issues and try to help them find solutions to their problems. The number for this service and other sources of help and information are listed at the back of this book.

Father figures

A recent study by the US National Centre on Addiction and Substance Abuse has shown that a child living in a two-parent family, whose relationship with their father is only fair or poor, is 68 per cent more likely to use drugs than teens living in the average two-parent family. Children in single-parent homes who have an excellent relationship with their mothers are 62 per cent less likely to take illegal drugs than those in two-parent families who have a fair or poor relationship with their fathers.

Action through knowledge

Accurate information about the drugs trade allows people to form their own opinions and make their own decisions about drugs issues. Having gained knowledge about the global drugs problem, they may wish to share this with others, by talking with friends or writing articles for the school magazine.

Organizing a school debate about drugs can also help people understand the issues. One group of students could, for example, present all the arguments and evidence for legalizing cannabis, and another group could give the arguments and evidence against legalizing the drug. Students could then vote for which set of evidence and point of view they found most convincing. Another way of exploring the issues around drugs is to act out a sketch involving someone being offered drugs.

Purchasing power

How we spend money can affect the world around us. Purchasing power could have an effect on the drugs trade if people choose to buy **fair trade** goods from the countries where drugs are grown. This would allow farmers there to receive a fair price for their products so they can make a living without growing illegal drugs.

Students who eat at the school cafe might have a choice of fair trade teas, coffees, chocolate and other foods. If not, they could suggest these to the school council.

Protest power

Young people have a right to clean and well-equipped leisure areas for playing sport, cycling or skateboarding. If these

Buying fair trade tea, coffee and other goods ensures farmers get a good price for their products and fewer farmers turn to growing illegal drug crops.

Group discussions at school can be a valuable way of sharing views and knowledge about issues relating to drugs.

are messed up with, for example, discarded syringes or other evidence of drug-taking, the police should be contacted. It is probably also worth writing to the local government and to local newspapers and radio stations, to raise awareness of the problem.

By paying close attention to what is written about drugs in local newspapers or featured on local radio or TV, young people can play an important part in ensuring the subject is dealt with in a fair way. If judgemental words such as 'junkie' are used or **stereotypes**, a letter,

email or phone text message could be sent to the editor of the newspaper, radio or TV station.

The drugs problem is not something only experienced by a group of people cut off from the rest of society: it is a deeply entrenched part of society today. Everyone plays their part – in the choices they make when shopping for goods (fair trade or not), in voting for politicians, or when supporting organizations that help fair trade practices. In these ways everyone can do something to try to minimize the damage caused by the illegal drugs trade.

49

Facts and figures

Statistics connected with illegal drug use are collected by a variety of different organizations around the world. These include international organizations such as the United Nations (UN), governments of individual countries and **non-governmental organizations (NGOs)**.

For example, surveys are carried out in which people are asked about their drug use. These may not give an accurate picture because people do not like to admit to taking illegal substances. Other figures recorded by police, customs officers and hospitals show how many people are arrested for drug-related crimes, and who gets ill or dies as a result of taking drugs. By recording these figures every year the trend in drug use and drug crime can be seen.

The UK

In a study of 11–15-year-olds in 2002 it was found that:

- 6 per cent of 11-year-olds had used drugs in the last year compared with 36 per cent of 15-year-olds

- 13 per cent used cannabis (the most frequently reported illegal drug) in the last year and 4 per cent had used **Class A drugs** (such as heroin and cocaine)

- 38 per cent had at some time been offered one or more drugs

- overall, boys were more likely to have been offered drugs than were girls (41 per cent compared with 36 per cent).

Sources: Home Office; Department of Health; DrugScope

The USA

Studies of drug use and drug-related crime in the USA have shown that:

- in 2001, 16 million people (that is, 7 per cent of the 229 million who were aged 12 years and older) reported using an illegal drug in the previous month; 27 million, in the previous year; and 96 million had used illegal drugs at least once in their lives

- the most common illegal drugs used were: cannabis (12 million users or 5 per cent of the population); cocaine (1.7 million users or 0.7 per cent of the population); and **hallucinogens** (including ecstasy and LSD) (1.3 million users or 0.6 per cent) of the population

- an estimated 61,000 (16 per cent) of people in US jails committed their offence to get money for drugs

- in 2001 over $4 billion was spent on drug law enforcement, and $2.5 billion on drug treatment programmes

- in 2000, a total of 19,698 people died of drug-related causes; this was up by 16 per cent on the 1998 figure of 16,926.

Source: US Office of National Drug Control Policy

Australia

Official statistics for drug use in 2001 showed that:

- one in five (20 per cent) 14–17-year-olds had used marijuana/cannabis in the last twelve months; 5 per cent had used amphetamines; 4 per cent had used ecstasy or related drugs; and less than 1 per cent had injected an illegal drug

- cannabis was the most popular illegal drug in 2001, with one in three people (33 per cent) having used the drug at least once in the past twelve months

- while Aboriginal and Torres Strait Islander people made up around 2 per cent of the Australian population in 2001, they were twice as likely to use illegal drugs as non-indigenous Australians.

Sources: Australian Drug Foundation and Australian Institute of Health and Welfare

Further information

Contacts in the UK

DrugScope
32–36 Loman Street
London SE1H 0EE
Tel: 020 7928 1211
email: info@drugscope.org.uk
www.drugscope.org.uk

Fairtrade Foundation
Room 204, 16 Baldwin's Gardens
London EC1N 7RJ
Tel: 020 7405 5942
email: mail@fairtrade.org.uk
www.fairtrade.org.uk

The Home Office
50 Queen Anne's Gate
London SW1H 9AT
Tel: 0870 0001585
email:
public.enquiries@homeoffice.gsi.gov.uk
www.feedback.homeoffice.gov.uk

Know the Score
Confidential information and advice from
the Scottish Executive – the devolved
government of Scotland, and its
partner agencies.
Tel: (freephone) 0800 587 5879
www.knowthescore.info

National Drugs Helpline, Northern Ireland
Tel: (freephone) 0800 77 66 00
www.ndh.org.uk

Oxfam
Oxfam Supporter Services Department
Oxfam House, 274 Banbury Road
Oxford OX2 7DZ
Tel: 0870 333 2700
email: oxfam@oxfam.org.uk
www.oxfam.org.uk

Talk to Frank
Confidential information and advice jointly
funded by the Home Office and the
Department of Health.
Tel: (freephone) 0800 77 66 00
email: frank@talktofrank.com
www.talktofrank.com

Traidcraft
Kingsway
Gateshead
Tyne & Wear NE11 0NE
Tel: 0191 491 0591
email: comms@traidcraft.co.uk
www.traidcraft.co.uk

Contacts in the USA

National Institute on Drug Abuse
National Institutes of Health
6001 Executive Boulevard, Room 5213
Bethesda, MD 20892-9561
Tel: 301 443-1124
email: Information@lists.nida.nih.gov
www.drugabuse.gov

Partnership For A Drug-Free America
405 Lexington Avenue, Suite 1601
New York, NY 10174
Tel: 212 922-1560
email: webmail@drugfree.org
www.drugfreeamerica.org

Contact in Canada

Canadian Centre on Substance Abuse
75 Albert Street, Suite 300
Ottawa, ON K1P 5E7
Tel: 613 235-4048
email: info@ccsa.ca
www.ccsa.ca

Contacts in Australia and New Zealand

Australian Drug Foundation
409 King Street
West Melbourne
VIC 3003
Tel: 03 92 78 8100
email: adf@adf.org.au
www.adf.org.au

The Australian Drug Foundation manages a confidential children's helpline:
Tel: 1800 55 1800
email: somazone@adf.org.au
www.somazone.com.au

The DARE (Drug Abuse Resistance and Education) Foundation of New Zealand
PO Box 50744
Porirua
Tel: 04 238 9550
email: darenz@xtra.co.nz
www.dare.org.nz

Other useful contacts

The European NGO Council on Drugs (ENCOD)
Lange Lozanastraat 14
B-2018 Antwerpen
Belgium
Tel: + 32 3 237 74 36
email: encod@glo.be
www.encod.org

Transnational Institute Drugs & Democracy Programme
Paulus Potterstraat 20
1071 DA Amsterdam
The Netherlands

Tel: + 31 20 662 66 08
email: drugs@tni.org
www.tni.org/drugs

United Nations Office on Drugs and Crime
Vienna International Centre
PO Box 500
A-1400 Vienna
Austria
Tel: + 43 1 26060 0
email: unodc@unodc.org
www.unodc.org

Further reading

Why Do People Take Drugs?, Patsy Westcott (Hodder Wayland, 2000)

Learn to Say No: Solvents, Angela Royston (Heinemann Library, 2000)

Learn to Say No: Cannabis, Angela Royston (Heinemann Library, 2000)

21st Century Debates: The Drugs Trade, Louie Fooks (Hodder Wayland, 2003)

Junk, Melvin Burgess (Gallimard, 1998)

Drugs, Anita Ganeri (Scholastic, 1996)

World Issues: Drugs, Jonathan Rees (Belitha Press, 2002)

Glossary

abuse
misuse something or use it in a way that has a bad effect; drug abuse is the excessive or habitual use of drugs

addict
someone who feels a physical or mental need to do something, such as take drugs

AIDS
acquired immune deficiency syndrome, a disease of the immune system caused by the HIV virus, which is transmitted in blood and sexual fluids

cash crop
crop grown for sale (to obtain money) rather than for use by the grower

Class A drugs
drugs classified as the most dangerous in the UK Misuse of Drugs Act 1971; for example, cocaine, heroin, crack, LSD, morphine, ecstasy and any Class B drug prepared for injection

Class B drugs
drugs classified as less dangerous than Class A drugs, but more dangerous than Class C drugs, in the UK Misuse of Drugs Act 1971; for example, amphetamines, codeine (a painkiller derived from morphine) and other weaker medicinal drugs derived from the opium poppy

Class C drugs
drugs classified as less dangerous than Class B drugs in the UK Misuse of Drugs Act 1971; for example, tranquillizers such as diazepam (Valium) and temazepam, mild amphetamines, some painkilling medicines and cannabis (from 2004)

dealer
person who buys and sells goods

dependence
reliance on or addiction to something such as drugs

developed country
wealthy country that is economically advanced

developing country
poor or non-industrial country that is trying to develop its resources

fair trade
trade in which fair prices (more than standard prices) are paid to farmers in developing countries for their products

hallucination
experience of seeing or hearing things that seem real but are not really there

hallucinogen
drug such as LSD that causes hallucinations (trips) and alters the way the user sees and hears things

harm reduction
drugs policy in which the emphasis is on reducing harm, involving accepting that some people will use drugs, no matter what penalties are in force, and finding ways to reduce or limit the damage to the drug user and other people

high
feeling of high spirits or euphoria (intense excitement or happiness) that is sometimes experienced after taking drugs

MDMA
methylenedioxymethamphetamine, the chemical name for the drug ecstasy

non-governmental organization (NGO)
organization that is not associated with any government, often a charity

paranoia
mental condition involving feelings of suspicion and distrust — a sense that everyone is out to get you, or to criticize your behaviour or actions

peer pressure
influence from one's peer group (people of the same age, status, etc.) to do something, such as try drugs

prohibition
banning or forbidding something, especially by law; during the Prohibition period (1920–33) in US history, the manufacture and sale of alcohol was banned

psychosis
serious mental disorder that affects the whole personality

Rastafarian
member of the Rastafarian religious movement, which began in Jamaica; members have strict rules about how to behave and dress, including wearing their hair in dreadlocks, the smoking of cannabis and the rejection of much of Western medical treatments

recreational drug
drug taken for enjoyment (rather than as a medicine), especially when socializing

rehabilitation
restoring someone to healthy, normal life; for example after a period of addiction to drugs

schizophrenia
serious mental illness in which someone cannot understand what is real and what is imaginary

sect
religious group with extreme beliefs (usually a subdivision of another, larger religious group)

sedative
drug that has a calming or soothing effect, used as a medicine to treat anxiety or pain

stereotype
oversimplified and fixed idea about a type of person, which does not consider individual personalities or abilities

stimulant
substance that speeds up brain activity, making people feel alert and full of energy

tabloid
newspaper that is dominated by sensational stories, headlines and photographs rather than serious news

trafficker
person who supplies or smuggles illegal drugs within and across different countries

trip
hallucinatory experience caused by taking a hallucinogenic drug, especially LSD

Western
living in, originating from, or characteristic of the countries of the West, in particular Europe or the USA

Index

Titles in the *Just the Facts* series include:

Hardback   0 431 16174 7

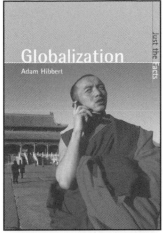

Hardback   0 431 16175 5

Hardback   0 431 16176 3

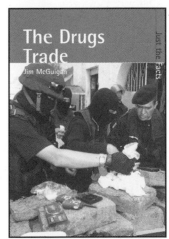

Hardback   0 431 16177 1

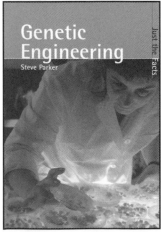

Hardback   0 431 16178 X

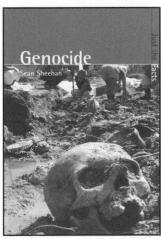

Hardback   0 431 16179 8

Find out about the other titles in this series on our website www.heinemann.co.uk/library